Old LARBERT and STENHOUSE[MUIR]
by Guthrie Hutton

Stenhousemuir Salvation Army Band in 1920.

© Copyright 1995 Guthrie Hutton
First Published in the United Kingdom, 1995
By Richard Stenlake Publishing, Ochiltree Sawmill, The Lade, Ochiltree, Ayrshire KA18 2NX
Telephone: 01290 700266

ISBN 1-872074-62-6

Staff at the Stirling District Asylum enjoyed many sporting activities including cricket. This is their team from 1896, soldiering on despite thirteen of their players being beaten by a Stenhousemuir Cricket Club eleven in 1892!

INTRODUCTION

The eighteenth century landscape north of the River Carron was dotted with great country houses and a scattering of humble cottages; a rural image as timeless as the changing seasons. But in 1760 the Carron Company, the greatest industrial concern that Scotland had ever seen, was set up on the Stenhouse Estate. Nothing would ever be quite the same again; villages grew and industry expanded until the big estates from Larbert to Carronshore were gradually swamped by a collection of communities, sharing the one urban mass, but each clinging to their own names and separate identities.

Larbert was perhaps the oldest village, nestling beside the Parish Church on the main road from Falkirk to Stirling. Suddenly, in the middle of the nineteenth century, it moved to the east, not because of some great seismic upheaval, but because the railway had arrived. In a few years Larbert had become the fulcrum of railway movements between Central Scotland and the north and beside the railway, sawmills and iron works were developed. Hospitals, needing good connections with the rest of the country, were established nearby too.

If the railway changed Larbert, it was the Forth and Clyde Canal that changed Stenhousemuir, not that the canal came anywhere near it, but when sheep and cattle, being driven to the great livestock markets known as the Falkirk Trysts, refused to cross the canal bridges the Trysts were moved from Rough Castle to Stenhousemuir. For a hundred years, thousands of animals were brought to the muir at sale time by Highland drovers. Lowland farmers came to buy, bankers were there to finance the deals and traders set up their stalls. The fairground today continues the tradition, but little else. Stenhousemuir grew along with the Carron Company and would probably have remained largely unknown, but for two things; toffee and football. As punters sought news of the football results, and with them that elusive treble chance, the name became known across the length and breadth of Britain. Highland Cream Toffee confirmed the village's existence. But while strangers puzzle over where it is; the burning question locally is, why is the football team called the Warriors?

East and West Carron and Carronshore were inextricably linked to the Carron Company, although Carronshore was a thriving harbour long before the great iron works was set up. The roaring furnaces and pounding hammers attracted huge numbers of people to seek work in the area and conditions in the surrounding villages deteriorated until, in the late nineteenth century, housing in Carronshore had become filthy and neglected with open drains carrying raw sewage past the front doors of damp, overcrowded houses infested with snails and cockroaches. The sylvan countryside had been replaced by industrial squalor!

Only a small element of the once great Carron Company now remains, but while the fires there, and in the numerous iron works of Falkirk, went out long ago, smoke still drifts across the village from Larbert's foundry. It has outlived them all. With much of the old industry gone, the area might have reverted to open countryside, but instead, housing is continuing to expand as the motor car and the semi-encircling motorways give people the opportunity to live in pleasant surroundings miles from the towns and cities where they work. This area of many communities and many names is not going back.

Guthrie Hutton, September 1995.

Underneath the arches, Larbert style. Road bridge foreground, railway viaduct behind.

The sight of a tram crossing an eighteenth century bridge in the heart of the countryside might seem faintly incongruous, but this rural section of track was part of a unique circular route created by the Falkirk and District Tramways Company in 1905. The route ran west from Newmarket Street in Falkirk through Camelon, along the Stirling Road and over Larbert Bridge here to the Cross. From Larbert Cross it went through Stenhousemuir to Carron where it re-crossed the river and returned to Newmarket Street through Bainsford and Grahamston; unless of course you went round the other way! This 'Circular' route is still followed by the number 90 and 91 buses today. The old bridge, seen here from beside the railway viaduct, is still standing but the traffic now uses a new bridge and realigned road.

The railway viaduct can be seen behind the road bridge in this picture which shows three forms of motive power together; horse drawn cart, electric tram and steam railway. The viaduct was built as part of the Scottish Central Railway which opened in 1848 between Greenhill and Perth and became part of the great Caledonian Railway in 1865. Two years later it was the scene of a distressing accident when a broken axle derailed the rear half of a cattle train which plunged into the valley below killing a number of the animals on board. The old road passed under the most easterly arch of the railway viaduct which was so low that the Board of Trade Inspector insisted that the Tram Company display signs above the arch to warn tram passengers not to touch the electric cable just above their heads.

The road and railway bridge builders were not the first to cross the river, that honour went to the Romans who built a road north through Camelon. It is thought to have crossed the river south of Larbert Parish Church and continued past it up the hill. The church was built in 1820 to the designs of David Hamilton the Glasgow architect who built Falkirk's town steeple. It replaced a seventeenth century building and was extended again in the late nineteenth and early twentieth centuries. The old manse, which predates the church by over a hundred years, still stands near the church beside the Denny Road. The publisher of this 1904 postcard, however, clearly thought the view of the church would look better with a cow in the foreground - so he stuck a rather obvious one on. The 'tongue in cheek' message on the back reads: "Isna that an awfu' bonnie coo?".

Old Mill on the Carron. Larbert.

This pronounced bend on the Carron is to the west of the church. The old mill beside it was powered by a lade that took water from the river nearly a mile away round the bend. The mill was bought by the Carron Company, one of a number of mills in the area bought by them and, as the Larbert Grinding Mill, was used to grind and polish iron grates. Extensive use of the river by industry caused heavy pollution that has only recently been cleaned up. On the extreme right of the picture is the lodge house of Larbert House. The present Larbert House was, like the church, designed by David Hamilton and built in the 1820's. The house and grounds were bought in 1926 by the Royal Scottish National Institution who built villas in the grounds to accommodate adult patients. The completed village was known as the Colony.

The Royal Forest of Torwood, to the north west of Larbert, is said to be a remnant of the great Caledonian Forest that once covered much of Scotland and it stands as silent witness to much of Scotland's story. Through it ran the Roman Road that crossed the Carron south of Larbert Church. William Wallace sought refuge here after his catastrophic defeat at Falkirk in 1298. The Scots army sheltered here from Cromwell's troops as they battered Callendar House in Falkirk into submission and the Jacobite army skirted it in 1746 as they marched from Plean to surprise the Government troops at the second Battle of Falkirk. This ruined sixteenth century mansion, known as Torwood Castle, was once home to Lord Forrester, The King's forester, but is now the subject of a one man restoration project.

THE OLD TOLL, TORWOOD, LARBERT.

The Castle is not the only defensive structure in Torwood. To the north of it is a broch, a large prehistoric circular tower 35 feet in diameter inside and with 20 feet thick walls. Brochs are normally found to the north and west of here and one so far south is unusual. What is also unusual is that no Roman remains have been found at the site which is probably more remarkable than if they had been found! The village of Torwood has no doubt, watched all this history unfold before it with the resigned disinterest of people watching world events on today's television news. It will have taken more than a passing interest, however, in the armies of Highland drovers on their way to and from the trysting ground at Stenhousemuir. These armies had money! The Toll House is seen here at the gushet, with the Stirling Road on the right.

The 2nd Stirlingshire (Torwood) Boy Scout group drew its members from all over the Larbert area. Their leader was Sir Ian Bolton Bt., who is seen here sitting fourth from the left in the second row from the front. The picture was taken near the Scout hut with the Glenbervie Golf Course boundary wall behind them. It featured in a painful initiation ceremony which involved new recruits being tipped off it into the nettles on the other side - if they didn't 'greet' they were 'in'. Sir Ian was wounded in the leg when serving as a Captain with the 3rd. Battalion, Argyll and Sutherland Highlanders during the First World War. The wound never properly healed and he walked with crutches thereafter, an impediment that didn't apparently affect his speed over the ground when chasing boys who intruded on his West Plean estate!

The Torwood troop was formed just before the First World War and was one of the most successful in the county, a success due in large part to the efforts of Sir Ian and his father, Sir Edwin Bolton, before him. The two men were very active in the Scout movement. Both were County Commissioners for Stirlingshire and Sir Ian was president of the Boy Scout Association of Scotland for many years. Here the Scouts, possibly during Sir Edwin's time, are lining the Stirling Road, as a mounted policeman (or soldier) rides between their lines. Sadly the occasion, and therefore the exact date of the picture, is unknown. The location is more certain; it is just north of Larbert Cross with the Commercial Hotel on the left and the Parish Church in the background.

The Commercial Hotel is on the extreme right of this picture of Larbert Cross looking south. The road has now been realigned and all of the buildings on the right hand side of the old road have been demolished to make way for the new. On the left, the Red Lion Hotel, still looks much the same today except that the cottage to the right has been replaced by the Carriage Restaurant. This picture from the 1930's shows the overhead tram wires still in place, but it is a bus, not a tram, that is heading up the hill from the railway viaduct. After the First World War bus services started to develop throughout the area and some competed directly with the trams. The tram company also operated their own buses under a subsidiary company, the Scottish General Omnibus Company, known simply as the 'General'.

The tramway company was taken over in 1920 by the Fife Tramway Light and Power Company who operated trams in Dunfermline. Throughout the 1920's they started to improve the system and by August 1929 the old Circular route had been completely modernised and new single deck trams introduced. But events overtook them. The Scottish Motor Traction Company bought the 'General's' great rivals, Alexanders buses, who in turn took over the 'General'. Six years later S.M.T. bought and closed the tramway, leaving the roads clear for Alexanders. The tram depot, or 'Car Sheds', off the Stirling Road at Carmuirs where this old tram is heading, became a bus garage. The picture looks toward the Cross and the Denny road from Main Street. The buildings in the background have all now been demolished.

When the tram tracks were laid in 1905 a complicated triangular junction was put in at Larbert Cross. It was apparently never used as an intermediate terminal and is thought to have been made to allow for future expansion of the system to Stirling. The tracks can be seen here in front of this tram heading anti-clockwise round the 'Circular' route and the children standing in front of it are certainly confident that it will go round the corner and not straight ahead. Across the road from the Red Lion, was the Wheatsheaf Inn which has a stone lion mounted on its gable wall. Apparently the lion slipped off a drunken carter's waggon one night outside the Wheatsheaf and the Inn's owner, or so the story goes, mischievously mounted it on the wall, adding confusion to coincidence for a time, by painting it red.

Next to the big tree in the previous picture was Bryce's Bonnington Dairy. Cows, kept in fields on the other side of the Stirling Road, were milked in the brick byre at the back of the cottage on the right. The upper floor was a hay loft. The wee shop was originally a cart shed, but was converted for the sale of milk, dairy produce, ice cream and Aberdeenshire eggs. Special crates were put on the morning train to Aberdeen, filled at the station there and returned to Larbert in the afternoon - now that's a railway service! The byre was used as an emergency feeding kitchen during the Second World War and the County Council prepared school meals in it until 1949. Barbara Davidson used it for her pottery before moving to the corner of Muirhall and Bellsdyke Roads and it is now used by the Carronvale Bindery.

Larbert Bowling Club, seen here from Pretoria Road, was established in 1873 on land granted by Sir John Graham of Larbert House. The conditions of the grant were reconfirmed in 1961 because until then the clubhouse lacked that essential ingredient for success, a bar. Success on the green came in 1905 when the club won the Scottish Fours Trophy. The club has also won the Stirling County Bowling Association's County Trophy three times and the Eastern District Bowling Association's Mitchell Trophy six times. In the early years one of the greens was used for croquet; the 'ladies' can be seen playing it on the far green. Apparently the croquet lawn was also used in later years as a putting green with weekly prizes of one shilling for lucky youngsters. Young bowlers are actively encouraged at Larbert and the club has a very successful junior section.

Youngsters like these have been enjoying the best years of their lives at Larbert Village School since it was opened in 1891. Two years after the opening a new wing was added and an infant department was built in 1904. Classes for pupils over the age of twelve were moved to Larbert Central, now Larbert High School, in 1928, but the infant school building continued to be used for various functions until 1972. It was put to good use during the Second World War when army units, including Polish troops, were billeted in the main block. The pupils at that time enjoyed extra 'holidays' to help with the potato harvest and later to celebrate the end of the War. Some famous former pupils include Hollywood comedy actor James Finlayson, international golfer Cathy Panton and Scotland footballers Bobby Brown and Kenneth McKenzie.

Opposite the Village School was the distinctive Stewartfield Buildings, the terrace seen here with the turreted corner block. It has now been replaced by four blocks of flats. The building on the left is the Nurses Home and between it and the terrace is Victoria Road. Eastcroft Street is off to the right beside the telegraph pole. The picture was taken before the tramlines were installed and before the packed stone and dirt surface of the road had been improved for motor cars. J & W Thomson's Muirhall Garage was between Stewartfield Buildings and the station. The site is still used by a garage and filling station. Thomson's also operated a hiring service from Muirhall Road where the '... comfortable and smooth running cars', came with '... careful drivers to ensure the maximum pleasure'. In the distance, on the left, is Station Terrace.

Station Terrace was built as a speculative venture by the Moscardini brothers who owned a number of cafes in Falkirk and made their own ice cream and ginger beer. They were convinced that Larbert, with its excellent railway connections, was about to 'take off' and thought that their imposing terrace would be in at the start of a property boom. They were wrong, and to make matters worse, the builders 'went off with the money' and the brothers had to borrow from the banks to complete the building. It then had to be sold off to clear the debt and the Moscardinis kept only the one fish and chip shop, on the left hand end of the terrace. It is still a fish and chip shop today. The top two floors of the tenement have now been remodelled, giving it a curiously hybrid look, but perhaps more in keeping with the scale of surrounding buildings.

Somewhat disenchanted, the Moscardinis left Scotland and returned to Italy, but financial problems seemed to stalk them, because the Lira collapsed and back they came to Scotland. There is still a Moscardini cafe in Manor Street in Falkirk, with wonderful interior woodwork and fittings. The fish teas are good too! Behind Station Terrace here is the Station Hotel which for many years was owned by a John McLay. When he died, his widow Agnes took over and in her time it was used for the formation of a number of sporting bodies. In 1884 the Stirlingshire Football Association was formed at a meeting there and a year later, at another meeting, the Falkirk Tryst Golf Club was formed. The Hotel later claimed to be the 'Headquarters of all Sports Associations in the Midlands of Scotland'.

Larbert Station.

Larbert was a meeting point for railways from all over Scotland. The line was originally laid by the Scottish Central Railway in 1848. It later became part of the great Caledonian Railway, although the North British Railway also had running powers over the track to Stirling and beyond. In time the Caledonian became part of the LMS and the North British part of the LNER. The original station buildings, seen on the front cover, were replaced in 1892, but the wheel has turned full circle and the station has now reverted to a more modest structure. Four tracks ran through the station, the inner ones were for through trains while the outer tracks served the main and north south platforms. The outside ends of the platforms were used for local trains and the south bound track can be seen in the right foreground here.

This busy and important looking northbound platform has now been reduced to an uncovered platform with a small waiting room. One of the busiest times for the station was when the Trysting Ground was used to assemble troops during the First World War prior to their departure for the front. It was from here that the ill-fated 7th Leith Territorial Army Battalion of the Royal Scots set off on 22nd May 1915 for the War in Gallipoli. They never left Scotland. An error by the signalman at Quintinshill, just north of Gretna, caused their train to smash into a stationary passenger train. Seconds later a London to Glasgow express ploughed into the wreckage. It was the worst railway accident in Britain; in the crash and ensuing fire over two hundred soldiers died. A plaque on the southbound platform commemorates that terrible day.

STENHOUSEMUIR, SOUTH EAST FROM LARBERT STATION.

The railway played an important part in everyday life in Larbert and businesses next to it learned to rely on it for more than just the transportation of goods. Shops were apparently opened and closed to the sound of passing trains. The tram tracks, seen here crossing the railway bridge, were laid throughout the system as single track with double track passing sections, one of which ran from the bridge to Burnhead Brae. The double tracks took up almost the whole width of the bridge, but it still had a footpath on the south side which has now been replaced by a separate pedestrian footbridge. The houses on the right here were all built before 1900, the large one on the corner of Main Street and South Broomage Avenue, is now the Larbert branch of the Clydesdale Bank. It is neighbouring Stenhousemuir, however, that gets the reputation for thrift.

These fine villas in South Broomage Avenue are the beginnings of the residential area of South Broomage that has mushroomed since they were built around 1900. They lost their view across the field in front long ago and Broomside Place now runs across the foreground of this picture. Although, as the Moscardinis had hoped, the railway was responsible for much of Larbert's property expansion, it was the advent of the motor car that really made a difference, particularly to areas like South Broomage which boasted one of the first three cars in Larbert. Many of the newly rich owners and managers of Larbert industry lived in these new South Broomage houses. One of the grandest was Torwood Hall. Its distinctive tower can just be seen half hidden amongst the trees behind the white house on the right.

Torwood Hall belonged to James Jones, founder of one of area's most successful businesses, James Jones & Son Ltd., timber merchants. The house is now used as an old folks home and is seen on the left here from the tree lined country lane that became Carronvale Road. To the right is the little Broomage Cottage, still tucked away at right angles to the modern road. With the development of modern housing to the south, the road has become wider and busier and the traffic noisier and faster. The old road was an important link between Larbert and Camelon. It led to the Dorrator suspension bridge over the Carron River, which was known to local youngsters as the 'swing bridge' because it shoogled when they walked across it. It was however a more convenient route over the river than the often impassable ford and stepping stones it replaced.

The imposing Beechmount House, further down Carronvale Road, was for many years the home of Major Robert Dobbie. He was perhaps the most influential man in Larbert in his day, a status reflected in his telephone number, Larbert 1. His influence and wealth came from Dobbie, Forbes & Company's Larbert Stove and Iron Works which he set up in the 1870's with James Forbes. The Company's cashier Dermot Campbell later set up the rival foundry of Jones and Campbell with timber merchant, James Jones. The house was split up into flats in the 1960's but now the garden too has been divided into plots and a number of private houses built on them; even the old coach house at the corner of the site now has a garden. The house still looks very much as it did when this picture was taken around 1908 although the impressive conservatory has now gone.

At the foot of Carronvale Road is Carronvale House. The house and estate were originally called Broomage, but while that name has become identified with large areas of Larbert, the new owner who bought the house in 1819 changed the name to Carronvale. He also added two new wings to the house and planted the trees that surrounded it. More alterations were carried out by George Sherriff after he inherited the estate in 1896. The Boys Brigade bought the house after the Second World War and now use it as a Conference and Training Centre and, since 1987, as their Scottish Headquarters. It has accommodation for sixty, a lecture room and a gymnasium. Outdoor sports include volley ball, lawn tennis and croquet, a game no doubt familiar to this group posing on the front lawn in the early 1890's at the time when the house was owned by Glasgow merchant John Bell Sherriff.

On its way past Carronvale House to Dorrator Bridge, Carronvale Road, at this point a tree lined track, crossed the Carron Lade over this decorative bridge. The lade was both wide and deep and ran in a wide arc south of Larbert between the town and river. It was cut by the Carron Company in the 1760's from a weir below Larbert Church to their works a mile and a half away. The power of water from the Carron River was a major factor in Carron Iron Works being set up where they were, but despite its industrial origins the lade became an attractive waterside walk. It led to the extensive Carron Dams, where the water was stored and which were also regarded as beautiful, not just by local people, but by the large flock of swans that inhabited them. Both lade and reservoirs are now drained and partly infilled.

The valley of the How Burn between Carronvale Road and Waverley Terrace is now boggy and overgrown, but for many years was the site of Broomagehall Nurseries. In 1902 the owners offered tomatoes grown in these greenhouses and honey from their own apiary. Pot plants, bedding-out plants and fresh cut flowers were also available along with wreaths, crosses and bouquets. A small florist's shop continues the tradition. The nursery site was developed in 1965 by Russell of Larbert as a showroom and depot for bottled gas. They called it Smithfield, after their old King Street premises. The houses of Waverley Terrace, a development that was never finished, are seen here above the greenhouses. On the extreme left is the back gable of the West United Free Church.

BURNHEAD BRAE, LARBERT.   A.6351.

The Church can be seen in the right background of this view of the area 'between the Braes'. The foundation stone for the church was laid in 1900 by Major Dobbie of Beechmount and the building was completed the following year. The church hall however had been built three years earlier and services were conducted there until the church itself was completed. The villas in the right foreground were completed not long before this picture was taken in 1937 and are very fine examples of the architecture of the period. The dip in the road in front of them is now filled by a filling station and caravan compound! The burn that caused the dip is the dividing line between Larbert and Stenhousemuir and so the church, and the impressive Dobbie Hall opposite, are in Stenhousemuir. The Hall was Major Dobbie's most significant contribution to the area.

The Dobbie Hall was opened in 1901 by the Duchess of Montrose. Streamers, flags and bunting decorated houses and streets, and the local Volunteer Company of the Argyll and Sutherland Highlanders provided a guard of honour. Everybody had a half-holiday. Since then it has seen everything from concerts to sales of work and political rallies to drama festivals, but in the 1980's it came under threat. Proposed conversion to a sports centre was defeated by local opposition led by Findlay Russell. In recognition of his efforts the small hall was named after him and in a nice echo of continuity the new Duchess of Montrose formally re-opened the new Dobbie Hall Complex in 1995. Beside the Hall is the old Library building donated by Andrew Carnegie. It is now used by Age Concern in conjunction with their more modern building alongside.

Masonic Hall, Stenhousemuir

To the east of the Dobbie Hall is the Masonic Hall, the prominent building pictured here in 1903, the year it was built. The scene has now been transformed by the raised and re-aligned road which caused Miller Place, the buildings on the left, to be demolished and gave the Hall and the adjacent Crown Inn, run by the Morrison family for over a hundred years, a sunken appearance. The sign on the gable of the Crown Inn also advertises the services of a Carriage Hirer who offered extensive stabling, pic-nic parties and cut price funerals. A seasonal speciality during the summer months was a circular tour in a four-in-hand coach from the Crown Inn round by Bonnybridge, Denny, Bannockburn, Stirling and Dunmore and all for two shillings (10p)! The Masonic Hall belonged to Lodge Carron 139 which was founded in 1767.

The Plough Hotel at the gushet formed by Main Street and King Street is a distinctive landmark in Stenhousemuir and it survives today despite considerable demolition around it to create the new shopping centre. The Plough has strong associations with Stenhousemuir Football Club; at one time its owner was president of the club (and president of the SFA) and when the club's grandstand burned down in 1928, the teams used the hotel as changing rooms. Behind the bus, coming along Main Street from the Carron direction, is the Larbert Central Public School. It was opened in 1886, taking over from the old Parochial and Public Schools. The original buildings were much extended as the school role increased and in 1946 it was renamed Larbert High School. The Palace, the local picture house, was just out of this picture on the right.

CENTRAL PREMISES

The Stenhousemuir Equitable Co-operative Society Ltd. was established in 1861 and these handsome 'Central Premises' were opened on the corner of what is now King Street and Tryst Way in 1889. The Co-op was a local institution where everything from a haircut to a ham and sugar to a suit could be bought. The grocery shop had a broad hardwood counter with drawers underneath where loose produce was stored. The walls were lined with broad shelves stacked with a wide variety of tinned and packaged produce. The Co-op's independence came to a sudden and stormy end at a meeting in Larbert East Church Hall in 1976 when substantial losses forced it to seek amalgamation with Falkirk and District Co-operative Society. The buildings are now mostly empty and disused.

The Co-op buildings might have got a new lease of life in the 1980's if an ambitious plan to dismantle them stone by stone and rebuild them at Bo'ness had been carried out. The Bo'ness Heritage Trust planned to recreate the old interior as an exhibit, believing (correctly!) that the unspoiled exterior was already a prime example of a shop building of its period. It is seen here in the left hand picture at the end of North Main Street, the old name for King Street. Beyond the Co-op all the buildings up to the Plough Hotel have been demolished. The Salvation Army hall was in the tall building and opposite, in the right hand picture, was Stewartfield, where Russell's Farm Products, the forerunner of Russell of Larbert, operated from 1943 to 1965. Stewartfield and all of the buildings on the right were cleared away for the Cannon Shopping Centre which was opened in 1980.

THE LIDO, STENHOUSEMUIR   B 8411

Crownest Farm was swallowed up by the expansion of Stenhousemuir, but while the farm has disappeared, the name continues as Crownest Park. It was laid out as a memorial to King George V and its central feature is the children's lido, a pond with sandy beach seen here in this picture from 1953. Children, whose parents were unable to afford a seaside holiday in those hard-up post war years, must have had a lot of fun making sand castles at this inland shore. Sadly the beach is now overgrown with weed and littered with shopping trolleys. In the background, on the bank above the pond, is a group of 'prefabs'; those ubiquitous little prefabricated houses made from asbestos sheeting that were put up quickly to cure the chronic post-war housing problem and which survived longer than intended.

By the late nineteenth century the cattle trysts were no more and the ground where the Highland drovers had brought so much activity and business became a golf course. In June 1885, a hundred years after the first tryst, eleven men, most of whom were associated with the Carron Ironworks, met in the Station Hotel to form the Falkirk Tryst Golf Club. In its first two years the club was faced with exorbitant rent rises that would have driven it out of existence had it not been for the intervention of a benefactor who ensured its survival. Ladies were admitted to membership in 1888 and the initial nine hole course was extended to eighteen in 1908. The new clubhouse was opened in 1893 replacing the wooden shed that had served until then. The sandy ground made the course very dry inspiring visiting links golfers to regard it as the best inland course in Scotland.

The course straddles Tryst Road, seen here looking north, and shares the eastern side of the road with Stenhousemuir Cricket Club. Cricket was very popular in Scotland at the end of the nineteenth century and Stenhousemuir was one of a number of local clubs (there were four in Camelon and at least one in Bainsford) but it has outlived them all to become one of the foremost clubs in Scotland. It has won numerous league and trophy competitions and had a number of players capped for Scotland. The cricket ground is in the distance, off to the right. The site of the two storey building in the right foreground is where A. McCowan and Sons now make their famous Highland Cream Toffee. The opening past the two storey building on the right is Gladstone Road which gives access to another of Stenhousemuir's 'institutions', the Football Club.

Stenhousemuir Football Club was formed in 1884 and 111 years later, in 1995, won its first trophy when the team beat Dundee United in the League Challenge Cup final. The club was elected to the Scottish Football League in 1921, but seven years later a fire destroyed the Ochilview Park grandstand and all the club's records. The new grandstand was built in such haste that the architect forgot to provide access to the seating - what would today's Taylor Committee on crowd safety think of that! In another 1920's incident with modern parallels a Bainsford bookie tried to bribe the Warriors goalkeeper, but he picked the wrong man and ended up in jail for three months. Perhaps the club's most conspicuous contribution to the game was to install the first floodlighting in Scotland. It was inaugurated in 1951 at a match against a Hibs team that included one of Stenhousemuir's most famous sons, Willie Ormond, who went on to become Scotland's International team manager. This picture shows the team in season 1935/36.

INSTITUTION ROAD, LARBERT.

This unhurried country road, called Institution Road, has now become the western end of the A88, Bellsdyke Road. The railings on the right are part of the perimeter fence of the Scottish National Institution for Imbecile Children which moved here from Edinburgh in 1863. The Institution was a philanthropic and charitable body receiving donations from, amongst others, Queen Victoria. Royal patronage continued with King George V, who gave the Institution authority to call itself 'Royal' in 1916. The Colony at Larbert House was established in the 1930's and when the National Health Service was set up, the Institution became a special hospital under the Western Regional Hospital Board and is now part of the Central Scotland Healthcare N.H.S. Trust. The original Institution buildings are now disused.

FEMALE SANATORIUM. S.D.A. LARBERT.

Stirling District Asylum was built three quarters of a mile to the east of the Institution to comply with an Act of Parliament of 1858 requiring County Authorities to make provision for the care of mentally ill people. At the time many of them were confined in poorhouses in conditions little better than prisons. Larbert was an obvious choice, as it had been for the RSNI, because its good railway connections meant that building materials could be brought to the site more easily as could food and fuel for the completed institution. People could visit their relatives more easily too. Fresh air and sunshine were regarded as beneficial for all patients but particularly those suffering from infectious tubercular conditions who were kept apart from other patients in special Sanatoria. Here the verandah which allowed female patients to sit out, sometimes all night, can be seen. There was a matching ward and verandah for male patients.

Problems with the gas and water supplies delayed admissions, but these were overcome by June 1869 and the first patients were admitted then. They came from West Lothian, Clackmannanshire, Dumbartonshire and Stirlingshire and the Asylum quickly became recognised in the field of mental health care as an efficient and well run establishment. A number of extensions to the original buildings allowed patients to be separated into three types of ward depending on the severity of their illness. This ward, one of two now used as the launderette and sewing room, is seen here, possibly in the 1890's, decorated and furnished in a comfortable and domestic fashion. Patients made handcrafts in the ward, but those who were fit enough, were expected to work; sport and other recreational activities were encouraged too.

Female patients worked in the sewing room while male patients had workshops, but outdoor work was regarded as being the most beneficial and so patients worked at the farm or looking after the hospital garden and grounds. Together the gardens and farm supplied milk, fruit, vegetables, tomatoes and other produce to the hospital kitchens which are seen here in the 1930's fitted with appliances made by another of the area's big institutions, the Carron Company. The gardens also supplied pot plants and flowers to decorate the wards, as seen on the previous page. After the Mental Treatment Act of 1930, the word asylum was dropped in favour of 'Mental Hospital'. The name has further changed to Bellsdyke Hospital and its role too is changing as the emphasis for people with mental health problems shifts from institutional care to care in the community.

KINNAIRD HOUSE, LARBERT.

Along Bellsdyke Road, to the east of the hospital, is Kinnaird House. The present house, seen here, was built in 1897 to replace an earlier mansion, that had been the home of Robert Bruce, a prominent church reformer and founder of the Church of Scotland. He was exiled after falling out with King James VI, but was allowed to return on condition that he remained within a three mile radius of Kinnaird and so, because he was unable to go out to preach, the people flocked to Larbert Church to hear him. No such ties confined his descendant James Bruce, who made his name as an African explorer when he discovered the source of the Blue Nile. During the Second World War Kinnaird was the headquarters of the Polish Army and after the war it was used to store hospital emergency supplies. Local businessman Findlay Russell bought it in 1977 and started the daunting task of repairing the damage done by official neglect and misuse.

Stenhouse is believed to take its name from a curious beehive shaped 'stone house' over 20 feet tall and 28 feet in diameter which stood on rising ground overlooking the Carron. It was known locally as Arthur's O'on (oven), but the origins and purpose of the structure are lost in the mists of antiquity. Early antiquarians were convinced that it was a Roman Temple and a monument of great value, but sadly we will never know what it was because Sir Michael Bruce, the laird of Stenhouse, knocked it down in 1743. He used the beautifully dressed stones to build a weir on the River Carron, but they were washed away soon after, and lost. Bruce was vilified by his contemporaries for this act of wanton vandalism. Alas, his seventeenth century mansion of Stenhouse, seen here, has gone the way of the O'on too - it was demolished in the 1960's.

Old Works, North Gate

Present Works, North Gate

Old Works Entrance Gate

Present Works Entrance Gate

Scotland had seen little benefit from the Act of Union and was still recovering from successive Jacobite rebellions when the Company of Roebuck, Garbett and Cadell was formed in 1759. John Roebuck and Samuel Garbett were already in business together. They made sulphuric acid in Birmingham and also in East Lothian where they formed a partnership with local merchant, William Cadell. The three men set about looking for a site for an iron works. It had to be close to supplies of iron ore, limestone and coal which, as coke, the partners believed would replace charcoal, then the main fuel used in smelting ore. Cadell preferred sites in his native East Lothian, but the two Englishmen wanted to build a works to rival the largest in Britain. Their vision and ambition brought them to search for a site near Bo'ness.

The other key ingredient in determining the site was water, both to provide power to the blast furnaces and access to the sea for shipping out the finished product. The River Carron was ideal. The Company obtained land from Sir Michael Bruce, the destroyer of Arthur's O'on, changed their name to the Carron Company and started to build the works. The first blast furnace went into production on Boxing Day 1760 and within six years another three had been brought into use. Local people resented the fact that many skilled men were brought from England to build and operate the works in those early years, but work was work and soon hundreds of people attracted by the prospect of employment were pouring into the area. West Carron, seen here beside the Carron Dams, was one of many communities that sprang up as the population of the area expanded.

Within ten years of the first partnership being formed, Samuel Garbett's son-in-law Charles Gascoigne, had manoeuvred the three original partners out of the Company or positions of influence and had taken over from William Cadell's son as manager. It was as ruthless an industrial assassination as any invented by the scriptwriter of a television soap opera. Gascoigne extended the water supplies and expanded the Carron Dams to ensure that the works never lost power, but one invention, the Carronade, dominated his twenty years in charge. The Company's early cannon were unreliable and its reputation suffered as a result, but the short-barrelled, large calibre mortar-like gun which could fire four times the weight of shot fired by conventional guns was an immediate success. It not only established the Company as a major supplier of naval guns, but set it on a course of prosperity that was to continue for over two hundred years.

Carron Bridge, Carron

Wm. Harley, Stationer, Falkirk

In that time the Company didn't just make guns, it made a host of iron products including pots and pans, gutters and grates, stoves and spades, and it spawned an iron industry that was to dominate the area. A major reconstruction of the Company in the 1870's saw the building of the newer blast furnaces on the previous page and the distinctive range of office buildings seen here on the far side of the Carron Bridge. But when the Company collapsed in the 1980's the block was demolished leaving only the central section standing isolated and forlorn. The bridge here was re-built in 1905 for the new trams and the picture appears to show the tracks already laid in the left foreground waiting for work on the bridge to begin. When the Carron Works was in full swing special tramcars waited outside for shifts to end and took workers home in both directions.

Unlike many workers in early industrial concerns Carron employees were not tied to the dreadful truck system whereby they were obliged to obtain provisions from the Company store. Carron employees were paid in cash and they also ran their own co-operative store. Married householders employed by the Company could become members and dividends were distributed half-yearly to them on the basis of their shareholding, rather than on the purchases made. If a member failed to buy sufficient produce from the store, however, the rules allowed for them to be fined or, if they persisted in default, expelled. The store was in existence in the 1830's, well before this picture was taken sixty or seventy years later. Whether the old rules still applied at the time is not known, nor alas is the exact location of this bakery.

Small ships used the River Carron long before the works were set up, but local ship owners, hoping to take advantage of the new trade, were thwarted by that man William Gascoigne. Before he became part of the Carron Company he set up a shipping company with his father-in-law to carry all of the Company's trade to and from the harbour here at Carronshore. Later, as Company manager, he cut a barge canal from the works to Carronshore and also improved the navigation of the river by straightening out two bends. It was still a difficult river to negotiate and Carronshore men became renowned for their boat handling skills. Carronshore lost its position as the principal port on the river with the opening of the Forth and Clyde Canal and the creation of new port facilities at Grangemouth. The old port is seen here in the 1880's.

BIBLIOGRAPHY

Ian Scott	The Life and Times of Falkirk, John Donald: 1994.
R.H.Campbell	Carron Company, Oliver and Boyd: 1961.
Lawrence Keppie	Scotland's Roman Remains, John Donald: 1986 (reprint 1990)
Alan W. Brotchie	The Tramways of Falkirk, N.B.Traction Group: 1975.
John C. Gibson	Lands and Lairds of Larbert and Dunipace, Hugh Hopkins: 1908.
Fiona McIntosh	Larbert and Stenhousemuir, Falkirk District Council, Libraries and Museums: 1990.
Peter Moulds	The Warriors, Stenhousemuir F.C.: 1984.
John Jenkinson	Gless Doors and Jeelie Pieces, Falkirk District Council, Libraries and Museums: 1984.
W.B.MacLaren	Larbert and District Guide, Victoria Publishing Co.: 1949.
R.W.Penn	Bellsdyke Hospital, a short history, Falkirk District Council, Libraries and Museums: 1986.

BOB McCUTCHEON and THE BOOK SHOP, STIRLING

This volume would not have been possible without the help and co-operation of Bob McCutcheon. He supplied the illustrations, much of the research material and some anecdotal gems that have all gone into this book. Bob is one of those people without whom this country of ours would be the poorer. He owns the Book Shop in Spittal Street, Stirling, one of the finest Antiquarian book outlets in Scotland, and well worth a visit!

ACKNOWLEDGEMENTS

When I was a boy, Larbert was, to me, a station on the railway line from Dollar to Glasgow. It has been a real pleasure to get off and explore this fascinating area that is in many ways Scotland in microcosm. Digging into what shaped it and makes it tick has been exciting and enjoyable, but the most enjoyable aspect of doing this research has been meeting so many friendly people. I must thank them all for so generously sharing their memories and knowledge with me. I feel sure that if they are a representative sample (as they say in opinion polls) I would be thanking the entire population if I'd had time to get round them all. I am also indebted to Willie Jenkins for bowling advice. I must thank too the staff at the Falkirk Library for their unfailing good humour and helpfulness. I am grateful too for the support of friends in the area who have offered advice and help, the mistakes are mine, not theirs.

McCowan's 'hielan' coo', as famous as the toffee it advertises.